The Rhyme G

"Mum," said Tom.
"Can we play
our rhyme game?"

"Yes, Tom," said Mum.
"What rhymes with **sock**?"

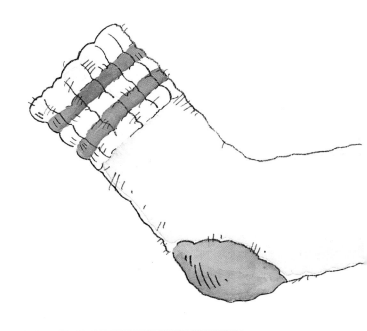

"Is it rock?"
said Tom.

S

3

Other words
that rhyme with sock:

dock

block

clock

flock

"Yes," said Mum.

rock

"What rhymes with **hat**?"
said Tom.

"Is it **cat**?"
said Mum.

h

Other words
that rhyme with hat:

bat

fat

mat

rat

"Yes," said Tom.

cat

"What rhymes with **cap**?"
said Mum.

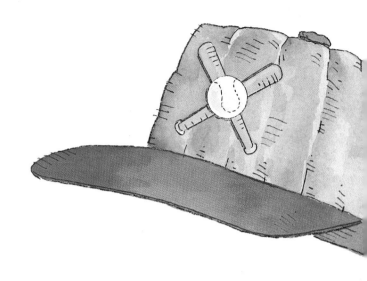

"Is it **map**?"
said Tom.

C

Other words
that rhyme with cap:

lap

nap

tap

sap

"Yes," said Mum.

map

"What rhymes with **log**?"
said Tom.

14

"Is it **dog**?"
said Mum.

Other words
that rhyme with log:

bog

fog

clog

frog

"Yes," said Tom.

dog

"What rhymes with **goat**?"
said Mum.

boat

"Look at that sign," said Tom.
"It rhymes."

Run and walk,
then sit and talk.

23

"And so do these words!"
said Mum.

24